EASIER SAID THAN DONE

ELIMINATING JUDGMENTS AND CHANGING OUR ATTITUDE

*To Margaret
With my best wishes.
Joanne Papper
3/4/99*

Missouri Publishing Company
P.O. Box 63411 • St. Louis, Missouri 63163

EASIER SAID THAN DONE

ELIMINATING JUDGMENTS AND CHANGING OUR ATTITUDE

Joanne Papper

EASIER SAID THAN DONE © Copyright 1998 by Joanne Papper. All rights reserved. No part of this book may be reproduced or transmitted in any form or any means, electronic or mechanical, without permission from the publisher, except by a reviewer who wishes to quote brief passages for a review written for inclusion in a magazine, newspaper or broadcast. For information address: Missouri Publishing Company, P.O. Box 63411, St. Louis, Missouri 63163

PRINTED IN THE UNITED STATES OF AMERICA.

Joanne Papper is a native of Missouri and has been writing for the past twenty years. She married at age seventeen and became the mother of four children, one girl and three boys.

Joanne found it hard to overcome the tragic death of Margie, her twenty-two year old daughter. Then, came the death of her mother; and following that, she was divorced after thirty-seven years of marriage. She lost her home and most material possessions.

EASIER SAID THAN DONE gives an account of how she coped throughout these trying times. Her suggestions to the reader are based on experience. The path she follows is one, which can be shared with those desiring a more peaceful life.

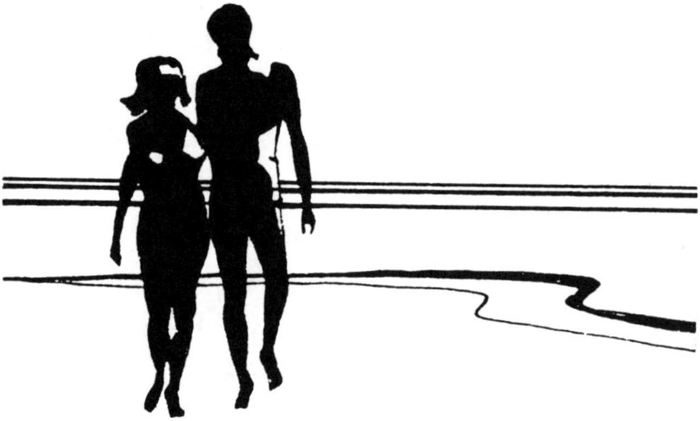

INTRODUCTION

When you were in school and the teacher gave you an assignment, what do you think her reaction would have been if you had said to her, "Easier said than done!" I can't imagine, can you?

Now that there is no teacher to keep you on track, who's running your show? And is that person doing a good job or just letting things slide? Ideally, we are in charge of our own lives; however, that doesn't mean we are satisfied with the way it has gone.

Speaking for myself, my life has not turn out as I had envisioned. There has been more sadness than I had ever dreamed. There were illnesses of family, self, and friends. There was an unhappy marriage and divorce, the death of my daughter, the sadness of which words cannot convey. Later, there was the death of my mother. Then, the loss of my home and most material possessions. Thank God for good health.

There's been loneliness; self blame, blaming others and more emotions than ever seemed possible. How are we expected to cope? I didn't have anything to work with except the will to survive. That came, only after realizing that I had one more child to raise.

Then, I found a new attitude. It looked good to me, but you know, it was easier said than done. I can be a very persistent person and when it comes to determination, if I don't have it, I can get it.

The first "someone" I asked to help me was God. Could you think of a better choice? You may call Him by any name you choose but I think we have the same Friend no matter what name we call Him. I knew that had to be the first step. Don't get me wrong; I'm not a church-going person by any means; but I am one of His children and He's here to help me. All I have to do is be sincere and ask. And after I ask, feel certain that he will help me. I have no doubts.

Everyone is right; it is easier said than done; it's just that it annoys me to hear it because I know that this particular statement is just a cop- out. I've used it many times. What are people really saying when they say that? They mean they don't want to work on it. They know it's hard to do. They are not ready.

One thing is for sure: People are where they want to be! And they're doing no more than they want to do. We know, because we all have done it. Funny, isn't it? We are all so unique------and so alike.

There are times, even now, that I still try to control my life when I know I've turned it over to God to handle. Nowadays, less time expires before I correct myself and give it back to Him. I must say He's more understanding and forgiving than my teacher ever was!

Attitude and judgments are inherent to those of us who like to see results go our way. We must consider that others have their own situations to work out. Their timing, and their wants, that's also important. The thing that gives us the most trouble is having our own agenda. Predetermining an outcome always presents big problems. It's a "no-no." Also, most of us are judgmental. We think we know how a person is, when we don't. We assume. We think we know the right way and the wrong way for others to behave, when we don't. We assume. We must concentrate only on our way of doing and being; then, we can leave someone else's business alone. This will bring a sense of relief that you will enjoy and so will those who have been under your "sentence". We are not the judge and jury of anything except our own lives.

Forgiveness plays a part in this also. It's not easy, but it is possible. You can't imagine how relieved you will feel by dropping that burden, your whole appearance will improve. The smile comes back, the wrinkles fade and you're fun to be around again. That makes it worth it! Try it! Even, and especially, your friends will like it!

TABLE OF CONTENTS

14......MARGIE
16......TO MARGIE
18......LOSE OR OWN
19......DEFEAT
20......NOTHING LOST
21......DAD'S THEORY
24......IMPORTANT
25......LIMITS
26......DO IT NOW
27......TRIAL AND ERROR
30......WORRY
31......WONDERMENT
32......THE BUCKET
34......GUCCI ® SHOES
36......WHAT
37......THE "PREVENTER"
40......THE COMPLETE CIRCLE
41......THE POOL
43...... HUMOR
44......YOUR CALL
45......WOE IS ME!
46......HENRY'S FRIENDLY TIP
48......SELFISH
50......COMPROMISE
52......RULES OF THE GAME
53......WHATEVER
54......PICKING AT THE SCAB
56......YOUR GIANT LEAP
58......THE ANT STORY

59.......OLD STANDBYS
60.......EXPECTATIONS
61......BETTY
63......HOPE
65.....THE FLOWER
66......IS GOD PUNISHING ME?
68......KEEP IT IN MIND
69......THIS MOMENT
70......PUTTING IT TO REST
72......THE ART OF LETTING GO
74......RELATIONSHIPS
75......PLAY ACTING
76......SINGLES
79......WHAT IS
80......THE KEY
81......TRY SUCCESS
82.......SUGGESTIONS
84......SOAPS
89......WHO DID IT?
91......GROWING PAINS
92......WHO WON?
95......YOU MIGHT ASK
98......FINDING YOUR BEST FRIEND
102....STAGE FRIGHT
103.....EXTRAVAGANZA
106....THE TOP 12 LIST
107....THINGS THAT TAKE FOREVER TO
          .LEARN
110....LIFE'S CHOICES
111....FRIENDS AND LOVERS
112....FIRST THINGS FIRST
113....FINDING A FOCUS

115.....OUR CHILDREN
116......MUTUAL
117.....INDECISION
118.....LOVE IS A CHOICE
119.....JOHN
124.....SO MUCH MORE TO SAY
125.....MOTHER AND DAD
128.....JUDGMENTS
129.....PRIORITY LIST
130.....OUTCOMES
131.....JOHN 13-34..
132.....THE KEYS
133.....BIRDSHIRT
134.....OUR FREE CHOICE
135.....OUR RIGHTS
136.....DISSAPPOINTED
137.....SPRING'S LESSON
138.....LIFE'S SONG
139.....MEMORIES
140.....MOTHER
141.....WHAT'S WRONG?
142.....DIRECTION
145.....TEDDY
146.....GET IT OUT
147.....CUTTING SLACK
148......ATTENTION
149.....TOMORROW
150.....TRAGEDIES
152.....LEFT BEHIND
158.....TO BEREAVED PARENTS

MARGIE

Twenty-two, blonde, beautiful, loving, kind, funny and very talented. On a lovely, August day she left our house on her way to an outdoor concert. I saw her leave at 5 PM. At 6 PM. she was dead.

Drunk drivers never know the repercussions from their lack of judgment.

Words are insufficient to tell you how I suffered. Truly, only those of us who have lost a child will be able to fully understand. I realized this fact six months later when I went to my long time doctor. He was a very educated, professional man and yet he said to me, "Aren't you over that yet?"
No, I wasn't. Never will I be "over that". That was a long time ago and I've since learned to live with it. Talk about something easier said than done, that was incredibly hard.

I wanted you to know a little about Margie, my life, my trials and tribulations, so you could understand where I'm coming from with my observations in this book. Believe me, they were lessons hard and many. But if just one other person could benefit from any of them it will have been worth the struggle to write this book.

After Margie died, my mother died, my marriage failed, and my divorce took four and a half years.

No Ph.D. for me, just life.

I hope you can take a shortcut resulting from one of my stories. If it's your time to, you will.

I remain,

Margie's mother.

TO MARGIE

I know for a fact, I'll see you again, you don't have to ask how I know.
Not an act of faith, not an inner knowing.
The angel came to me, said he talked to you, "The girl with the golden hair".
You sent him to me, I was lost in utter despair.
Not living, not dying and worst of all, I didn't care.
Yes, lost is the word.
Lost in a place I'd never been, a place of No More.
It was the movie of my own life, stuck between frames without action.
I was safe, where nothing could happen.
Then when your messenger came, he explained that you had talked with the "Great One" concerning my resignation.
What else could I do? All hope was gone, my child had left before her time.
It would take an act of God to bring me back to face this world again.
You know me well.
As I listened to your messenger's words, hope returned; the purpose of events, the bigger picture of our existence became clear.

The movie of my life has continued on, frame by frame. And in the end, I know I will see you, again.

LOSE OR OWN

You do not "own" anyone or any thing in this life.

You can not lose what you have never owned.

DEFEAT

Failure acknowledged, is the first step to a new beginning.

Given time, we see that our failures are actually our gain in disguise.

NOTHING LOST

At the end of a relationship I consider the positive viewpoint. We have made progress with discovering the joys of caring. In the past, we had experienced loneliness and remedied that with sharing. We bravely opened the door to our heart and let another person in.

Even though we chose to close the door on our relationship, we are that much closer to finding our true needs.

In most situations, each "Hello" marks a new beginning. Each "Good-bye" marks advancement. Nothing is lost. And what we have gained will soon surface.

DAD'S THEORY

It's a cold, rainy November day ----a perfect day to remember my life at age sixteen. One morning, Dad was teaching me to drive and wanted me to practice by taking him to work.

Nervously, I backed out of the driveway, full speed in reverse. The brand new car sped across the road and hit our neighbor's giant oak tree. We stood looking at the damage, shocked at the sight of the rear end. Dad said, " Now get in and drive me to work."

He said no more, no less. He wasn't angry, his expression never changed. His theory was not to let anything stand in the way of what you wanted to accomplish.

We learn the hard way much of the time---- and this was going to be one of those times. I drove him to work, then forgot the lesson. I couldn't know how long it would take me to learn this one----- and it's good that I didn't.

On this cold, rainy day I reflect over my many years here on earth, trying to survive the heartaches that have come my way. As most of us know, we must learn a lesson or for sure we'll get it over again until we get it right. I'm trying again, but this time I can see that I'm on the right path.

Naturally, I don't want to put myself at risk again; but, this time I will. Unyielding self-protection has caused me endless heartache. Every time I get close to having really good people in my life I push them away. By being safe I've isolated myself from those who care for me. It's a definite pattern and one that must go. Now is the time to change my ways and the fight is on. Common sense tells me the right answers, but doing it is hard. My fears are very, very strong. They've become my enemy.

Some time ago, I found the courage to hand it over to a Friend of mine, absolutely. Many times, I'd tried before, but I'd quickly take it back. This time I gave in and realized that I'd made another mess of it. The pattern seemed to have no end. Each day has been a new day, sometimes not running smoothly---- but not to worry ---- because He's been very successful in making it all come out right. Right is not always what I think it should be, but look at my track record! You'll find that when you take your hands off of the control button wondrous things happen because He's capable of wondrous things.

Yes, you can bet it's hard to let go, but finally, I became convinced that my way was not productive. I hope that my kids will listen; however, I'd bet that they too must learn the hard way. That's called ----life.

My life has changed for the better. It may not be perfect and that's fine. I am looking for peace ----not the "fairy tale-come-true" that's painted all pinks and yellows---just a good mix of people, kindness, love, giving and sharing----and yes, learning.

IMPORTANT

Whenever you're faced with a problem and you can't seem to arrive at an answer, try this:

Take yourself out of the picture and replace yourself with someone you don't know. First, listen to this person relate the same situation with which you're concerned. Magic! Now, give your advice. You have the correct answer. The solution appeared.

When our own emotions are involved, the water gets very muddy and we can't get the true picture. Take away the overpowering emotions and our involvement, and truth returns.

LIMITS

You are the only one who can set limits on your life.

Don't!

DO IT NOW

Have you ever noticed some of the elderly people that you know seem to grow more loving as the years pass by? They no longer have to hit it every day. They have time to really notice people and the world around them.

Early days are filled with schedules, responsibilities and material expectations; latter days hold time for contemplation and appreciation for the wonder of life. Innocent childlike ways were lost in the struggle to succeed. Time was at a premium. For the older people, their lives seem to have flown by, unappreciated.

What a shame we can't grasp the importance of loving and being loved early on, and successfully hold on to it. Life would be simpler.

Too smart too late? No, it's never too late to enjoy, as long as you're smart enough to do it now.

TRIAL AND ERROR

Trial and error is usually the way we approach the things we're trying to correct. It is important to become who we want to be. We want the best for ourselves. If only we knew how to get it, and quickly at that! It's not that easy; however, it's not as hard as we have imagined. Nothing could be that hard!

A few years ago, I was very intimidated by the computer. I hadn't taken typing. I didn't have a great education, on and on. I thought, there are six year olds who use the computer, why couldn't I? (Oh, we do limit ourselves!) We do it all the time.

Fortunately, I faced my fear and bought a machine. Facing our fear is what we have to do if we really want to accomplish something. The end result was: I felt good about myself. At the computer supply store, I see people---- older than I am---- who have done the same. Through trial and error I've learned how to beat intimidation.

We need courage and self-esteem to succeed. We don't need to listen to negative remarks that may come our way when we express what we are hoping to accomplish. How could they know? We don't know ourselves---until we try!

Getting one's life in order is no small task. Make a start! The alternative:

You remain to be the same unhappy person that you *think* you are now.

Go back and read that word THINK. Your thinking forms your attitude and your attitude guides your life. If you are a negative thinker, your experiences tend to be negative. If you are a positive thinker, most experiences are positive.

To make your life more pleasant you will have to break old habits. That's the hard part! However, you can do it if you become aware each time you backslide----then, correct it. As you can imagine, this takes awhile. You will be unhappy with yourself for forgetting from time-to-time. But you'll grow in happiness as you see yourself change!

Are you seriously concerned about having a better life? Are you tired of wasting time? Are you dedicated? If not, stop here. If you are, then read on, with my best wishes to you. It's easier said than done, but you already know that. Give God a call and ask Him to help you. He will. Remember?

"Ask and you shall receive."

You can't receive, if you don't ask.

WORRY

This is where we hear "Easier said than done" It's so true! A habit is hard to break, especially if you're enjoying it!

Enjoying it? Do I really enjoy it? I must be getting something out of worry or I wouldn't spend so much time doing it. Maybe it's a process to work things out. No. It's not that. Rule that out. Maybe this, maybe that.

Could it be eliminated by staying in the moment? Uhmmm, maybe! Now lets see, if I don't worry about the past and I don't worry about things that haven't happened,

Question: Where am I?
Answer: I'm laughing at myself for being afraid of the future. I'm laughing at myself for holding on to the past. All that time wasted. Now, I'm not laughing!
What's happening now? In this very moment I could start to stay in the now where I'll find peace.

WONDERMENT

Wonder what's in store for next week?

Wonder if I'll like it?

Wonder if I could change it?

Wonder who could?

Wonder if I'd want to?

Wonder when it'll quit raining?

Have you been here and done that?

THE BUCKET

There are excuses we make when an impossible situation doesn't get better. We say it's going to be "all right". We then convince ourselves it's true. One excuse is: Things are going to get better. Long ago, I heard this story, and it's food for thought.

In a small, foreign town there was a large water fountain in the center of the square. One day, a young man noticed an old man walking up to the fountain carrying a bucket in his hand. (There was a foul odor about the man.) He didn't fill the bucket, just looked around---- and walked away.

Two weeks passed, repeating the same events. Finally, the young man approached the old man, looked into the bucket and saw that it was full of manure. Curiosity got the best of the young man. As he was about to leave he asked, "Pardon me sir, I'm wondering why you're carrying that bucket of manure?"

Offended at this rude remark, the old man looked him right in the eye and said, "Well --------I'm waiting for it to turn to gold! "

GUCCI ® SHOES

Our courthouse is located in a nice business district surrounded by lovely homes. There are office buildings occupied by attorneys, investment brokers and other business people.

This particular fall day, I had just come from my attorney's office and was entering the elevator. As the door opened I saw three young men standing and looking up at the ceiling. Obviously, boredom had set in.

Shoes tell a lot about people. Two of the men started talking to each other while the third was silent. The two men wore suits and the silent man wore casual slacks. Looking at their shoes, and pointing to the silent man, I said, "You all have the same shoes on, except your pair doesn't have tassels," The silent man smiled, pointed to the other men and said,

"Yes, but they're upper echelon!"

We all looked at each other and laughed.

Out we went into the sunny, September day and I thought about how silly we can get. Do we know what's important or not?

Save your money for a rainy day. Put some aside for a special treat. It may make life more interesting. Or, if nothing else, it may afford you an unexpected illusion!

WHAT

What color are you?
What religion are you?
What school did you attend?
What kind of work do you do?
What title do you hold?
What kind of car do you drive?
What kind of house do you have?
What does it matter?

Have you had your share of love in this lifetime?
How much love have you given?
That matters!

THE "PREVENTER"

Fear has made me feel unworthy.
I choose to accept God's love for me and His will for me to succeed in all things.
Fear has made me take things too seriously.
I choose to accept being imperfect, laugh at my mistakes and try again.
It has made me accept myself as I am.
I choose to be better than I have ever been.
Fear has made me afraid of having too much happiness.
I deserve much happiness.
Fear has made me accept boredom.
I will live life to it's fullest.
Fear wants me to lose my individuality.
I will let myself and others see who I really am.
Fear has made me afraid of rejection.
I am not a coward.
Fear has kept me silent.
I must be heard.
Fear has made me invisible.
I must be seen.
Fear has made me cautious of the love I feel.
I will love.

Fear has put me in limbo.
I will move on.
It wants me to hold on to the past.
I'll live in the now.
It has made me lonely.
I will love and be loved.
Fear wants me to make judgments of others.
I choose to have more understanding.
It has made me hold on to my feelings.
I choose to give and receive them.
Fear wants me depend on others for my happiness.
I will create my own.
It has made me look to others for forgiveness.
I will forgive myself, totally.
Fear wants me to believe it is powerful.
I refuse to give it that power.
Fear wants me to expect bad outcomes.
I will not dwell on outcomes.
Fear wants me to believe in failure.
Failure can teach a lesson.
Fear has made me deny my power.
I am powerful and I will use it wisely.
Fear has made me say no to the things I want from life.
I choose to say no to fear.

And I will do these things every day until I regain control of my life.
I recognize the enemy.

THE COMPLETE CIRCLE

What we presume to be life's errors may well be life's challenges, in disguise.

Out of disappointment and sorrow comes knowledge.

Out of knowledge comes Grace.

Out of Grace comes peace of mind.

Out of peace of mind comes the Secret of Life.

THE POOL

It was a beautiful summer day, the end of summer and just about the time of year that we wonder; where did the time go? No one was around the pool in our apartment complex when I got there. After 15 minutes or so a lady showed up carrying a book and a small raft. Then, the young Frenchman came along and also another man with a small boy. Not much of a crowd for such a lovely day.

The Frenchman, the lady and I were sitting around the pool watching the man with the little boy playing in the water. Suddenly, the woman jumped up from her chair. A bumblebee had landed on her and she was trying to get away from it. The Frenchman said to her, "Put your tongue between your teeth and bite softly."
She didn't know what to think about his advice. However, she tried it and the bee flew away! I had never heard of such a thing. My curiosity was aroused and I asked, "How did you know that?"

"I've always known that!" he said.

We all laughed out loud at the oddness of what had transpired. What fun! Naturally, the conversation went on with him explaining the reasoning behind his advice. "You see, that sets up electricity all over the skin on your body, which chases the bees away."

The rest of the afternoon the lady floated on her raft while sticking her tongue between her teeth. She looked at us and said, "I don't understand this but it works. I just figure.....whatever works!"

HUMOR

Although your life may be decorated with minor and major problems, try to remember this:

Humor is salve for life's bruises.

The directions read:

Apply freely---- as needed.

YOUR CALL

When you get up in the morning, you have two choices:

Happy or Sad.

Knowing this, how long will it take to make your decision?

WOE IS ME!

The only person I can change is me!

The only one I could blame is me!

Me-----going to change my
        attitude!

HENRY'S FRIENDLY TIP

Often, a fortunate choice of words can drive home a message. This was the case when my friend George, returning from an estate sale, ran into Henry, one of his long time competitors. They both sold merchandise to antique dealers around town.

"Did you find anything at the sale?" Henry asked.

"No" George replied. "And I got there when they opened the doors."

"I just came from there. Take a look in my car", Henry said. George couldn't believe his eyes. The wagon was loaded with a bronze chandelier, furniture, cut glass and much more. It was bursting at the seams. He stared at Henry, bewildered by what he saw. It was incredible! How did he manage that? George didn't even try to guess. Things always seemed to work for Henry.

Thirty years later, Henry's advice remained the turning point in George's personal and business affairs. Henry had said, "George, you're not asking for enough."

SELFISH

"Selfish" can be a confusing word. Usually it connotes the act of being stingy, however, that's not always the case. Sometimes I keep things I have duplicates of and others need. That's selfish. Other times, I give away things I love! That's okay, they need it more.

There was a time when I gave away myself. Now, that's not being selfish, that's being stupid. My excuse was, I didn't want to make waves that would drown me. I kept everyone else's priorities above mine and forgot to include myself. Somewhere on the list I knew there could be a place for me....but when? This made for an unhappy existence. Mine.

Years later, I came to my senses. I knew that I had to become selfish with my goals, my time, my needs and my life. I haven't thrown away the people I love; they're still on my list, but in their proper place. My place is at the top of my list, because, you know what? I can't love and do for others until I'm happy for me. I didn't know that was the criteria that must be met, but it is. We find it hard to easily give freely to others when we're unhappy about our lot. Sorry, that's just human nature.

If you're not first on your list consider moving up. Move to the top and make yourself comfortable enough to give to others without begrudging it. It works!

COMPROMISE

Another word with double meanings. You can compromise with people and that's fine. You can compromise yourself, and that's where you've made a big mistake.

The thing about compromising yourself is that it creates a whole new ballgame. There's only one player and he's cheating himself!

Maybe he compromised himself for love, money or one of his many ambitions. Whatever the case, he now has to deal with those terrible feelings that follow this action. Now, he's worried about what it is he did wrong. At least he knows he did something wrong!

Our conscience always tells us when we've done something against our beliefs. But, it doesn't tell us how we could have made a better choice.

It's important to know that all things happen for a reason. Maybe it's a lesson to be learned or maybe it's an opportunity for better self-understanding. You've probably done this one before and if you didn't learn the lesson, now may be the time to give it more of your attention.

The question may arise as to what you value most. Was it your own self-worth (and feeling good about yourself) or was it what you gained from the compromise?

It's honesty time and no one's looking. Can you give yourself an honest answer? If you can't stand being honest with yourself, who in this world could you possibly trust?

RULES OF THE EASIER SAID THAN DONE GAME

1 Stay in the now.

2 Work only on what belongs to you. Don't borrow someone else's problem.

3 Be aware of your negative thoughts and change them to positive, immediately.

4 Be aware of backsliding and correct it immediately.

5 Hands off of the outcome.

6 Truly, turn it over to God and know that He will handle it.

7 Don't take it back.

This will make a difference.

The difference is----peace of mind.

WHATEVER

Why did I get into the habit of saying "Whatever?" I imagine it's my way of saying that I have no control over the situation in question. The truth is, I've learned that I have little control over a lot of things. For instance: Your life, my grown-up children's lives, my grandchildren's lives, my neighbors' business's, my friends likes and dislikes, just to name a few.

Somehow, I've been more at ease since I've given up trying to arrange things for others. They didn't seem to appreciate it anyway..........whatever.

PICKING AT THE SCAB

Things happen, don't they? Nothing stands still very long, including the emotions we feel. Some days we're so happy we can hardly believe it and in the blink of an eye it can change. There are also the dark days that seem to last forever. Nothing lasts forever, thank God.

There's always life after the storm. It may be death, illness, divorce or any one of countless scenarios that come to mind. You name it------it could happen to you or me.

Many of us have survived extremely challenging times, resulting in varying degrees of damage. There may be scars that need to heal. Just as we must not pick at an old scab, we can avoid long, unproductive preoccupation with the past. Old wounds that don't heal are a threat to our health and happiness. We know this. Then why do we forget and continue to do it? For one thing, we're human.

A friend once said to me, " But I've been so terribly hurt in the past." He was referring to three years prior when his romance had broken up, and it sounded like he was right there in the throes of it all again. I answered him with a seemingly cold and sarcastic response: "Tell me, who has never been hurt?" Why do we think we're in the boat alone? We all do. In reality, the boat could well go down faster than the Titanic if we put everyone in there that has gone through hard challenges.

The way out of this situation may be harder to find than the exit in the house of mirrors, but it's there behind your self-centered reflection. When you can see beyond your own saddened image, you will find it. Stop picking at the old scab and get on with your life. Time's- a- wasting!

Been there, done that, seems appropriate here. Those of us who have been there, understand and welcome you to safe ground.

YOUR GIANT LEAP

How many times have you forced a situation to work out the way you think it should, only to have it fall on it's face? You know exactly what I mean because we've all done it, many times. We don't always learn fast. But sooner or later, hopefully, we do catch on. When you know that it's in God's own time and not yours, things get a lot easier. There have been times when I've asked Him, "What's your idea of time? Will it be in my lifetime?" (See what I mean by "Putting up with me"?)

I noticed that I only made things worse by imposing time limits on situations. My mind said, let's go with this now, get the show on the road, time's- a- wasting. What I forgot to consider is, there's always someone else involved in the situation and I didn't consider anyone else's schedule. Rome wasn't built in a day. I wasn't building Rome, I just wanted to have my own way!

After many total disasters, I have grown

to have more patience and understanding. I remembered how badly, forced issues turned out. It's been pointed out that if I let God handle it, in His own time, it works.

Children want what they want, when they want it. Adults sometimes revert back to childish ways. We aren't perfect and no one knows this better than our Friend who looks out for us and has a plan decidedly better than anything we could imagine.

You'll probably never make it in one leap or in twenty; however, you will see results when you can let go of your own strong will. When you remember this, know this and live with this truth, you've made your giant leap.

THE ANT STORY

Becoming so preoccupied with yourself and your work, is not the ideal way to enjoy life and those you love.

Remember when you were a child, the first time you saw ants frantically swarming around a crumb? Back and forth they go, busy with whatever their job entails. They never stop; they're dedicated. Being so engrossed with their numerous trips, they're not even aware of you observing them. In other words, for them, you do not exist!

People can sometimes form the habits of ants and too bad if you're close to them, for you're not in their plans.

There's no future for you with them. Remember, you do not exist. People long to be appreciated, don't you?

OLD STANDBYS

So often, advice that's given is a repeat of the old sayings. The one that annoys me the most is "You made your bed now lie in it."

You would be surprised how many people hold to that line of thought. For the most part, these people are past middle age. Young ones are having none of that. I feel this advice wasn't good in the first place. If you try to work things out and you try very hard and can't make it, then it's reasonable to scrap it if it's destroying your life and your peace of mind.

No one enjoys living with a martyr. Furthermore, it's no life being the martyr.

EXPECTATIONS

Expect much from yourself,
less from others
and nothing from material
possessions.
Life will never disappoint you.

BETTY

My friend Betty had just returned from taking her grandson to a large, famous clinic to see what the doctors could tell her about the child's health. It was not good.

My phone rang that night and it was Betty, devastated. She told me the details of the trip and also the outcome. Then she said, "They tell me there's little hope that he will ever be healthy. You can't take people's hope away, you just can't. I want you to write something about hope."

That was a tall order, since I knew that she would expect it right away. I had paper and pen and little else, since I was staying in the guesthouse in her back yard. I had left my husband and had no place to go. Things were not good, all the way around.

Here's what I came up with. I hope it will help someone, as I had hoped it would help Betty. She's never forgotten that evening and neither have I:

HOPE CONTINUED ON PAGE 63

HOPE

Hope is the very essence of life; without it we have little reason to go on. In all unfortunate situations the flicker of hope is what lights the fire of life. Poverty and illness can be tolerated with only a small amount of this life sustaining force to carry one through. It is only when we concede that hope is gone that the life force fades away.

This is why we mourn when someone we love dies. We feel that hope has made a final exit. But even in death there's hope for those who believe that death is a new beginning.

Hope is not tangible and therefore can not be taken away from you. Hold tight to your own beliefs. Hope is your protection from the adversities in life and it is the promise of tomorrow. Hope is truly the fuel of the flame of life. Continued.....

This happened in 1985 and Betty's grandson is still with us. He's not the perfect child-----(thank God). He lives, he loves, and he adores his grandmother. What more could we ask from a "hopeless case"?

THE FLOWER

Life is like the lovely flower that blooms on my patio for only one day. It's here for me to enjoy, but if I'm not paying attention, I miss it.

The next day, there's another blossom and another chance. It's here, I'm here. To take notice-----or to turn away is solely up to me. I can look at it as just another thing to care for, or I can look at it in awe of its fragile, simple beauty. It's my choice.

It's here, I'm here. Could it be that only my attitude and judgments determine my experiences in life?

IS GOD PUNISHING ME?

Toni's husband Jim was very ill and had gone through six major operations in a row. Jim had been such a good husband, father and friend, no one could understand why these things had to happen to him. Jim couldn't figure it out either. He was not one for the pity pot but now he was feeling very confused.

Every morning before Toni went to see him she prayed for the right words to bring him out of his depression. He had been through so much and really hadn't complained. Now he looked so terribly down; it hurt to see him that way.

They had been together so many years, through a war, raising children and working for their dreams. If only God would tell her how to handle this terrible letdown. Jim needed her; she felt so helpless.

This particular morning as Toni was sitting by Jim's bedside in the hospital he said, "Why is God punishing me this way, Toni?"

Toni answered very quickly and firmly. "Don't flatter yourself, Jim. What makes you think He would single you out just to punish you? My God and your God is the same God and He doesn't punish, He loves people."

Toni said Jim's eyes were as large as silver dollars. He was absolutely shocked. She had gotten the reaction she had hoped for. She knew God gave her those words for her dear husband and it worked.

After going through a bypass and a partial amputation of one leg Jim is now walking three miles each day and working out. No one around him on his workouts is aware of his trials.

Amazing? Yes. God is amazing. Ask and you shall receive. Believe it will be done and it will be done.

The outcome will be God's will. It may vary from your expectations, but it will be the help that is needed.

KEEP IT IN MIND

Life is like the river, always flowing, always changing. Not one of our days is an exact duplicate of a previous day.

Tomorrow hasn't happened. Enjoy today; don't worry about things that do not exist. It's called: Staying In The Now!

THIS MOMENT

In this moment, you can change your life forever.

Believe that you deserve happiness.

Want it,

allow it,

then enjoy

what is rightfully yours.

PUTTING IT TO REST

There are several options when another wrongs you:

1. Fight back.

2. Hold it in.

3. Forgive but don't forget.

The first two are the most popular, however, they're also the most harmful to you. The last is easier said than done, so it follows that it is also the most beneficial.

I have tried them all in the order that they appear. Forgiving has two sides to it and initiating it is difficult. I decided to pray for the person who did me wrong. I needed help, so I asked God to assist me in getting the words out of my mouth. I must admit that I had selfish reasons. I wanted more peace for me. The part about not forgetting is simple. It means to remember not to let it happen to you again. After I prayed for this person, I felt good. Simple as that.

I had spent a lot of time thinking about what this person had done to control me. Then, I realized that he was still in control, only when I dwelled on it.

It was time for me to catch on to the game and put this issue to rest. That's when I won!

Know anyone playing this game?

THE ART OF LETTING GO

Like the subtle changing of the river and the clouds, all things change.

They follow their own distinctive course.

Accept it and let things and people come and go, as they will.

We have so little control.

Easy to say and hard to do?

I hear you. Yes, it's true.

But accepting is when you're holding the ace.

Let go of ambitions and desires. Still your ego.

God gave us free choice for this time and space.

Would you hold back the river or control the clouds?

Tell me.

How?

RELATIONSHIPS

What is love?
Someone must know!
I believe it's a choice we make.
But from where does it grow?
Emotions are important, I know.
Someone must have the answer,
besides God above.
When it comes to choosing a mate....
how do you know?
In the end, I won't settle for less.

Shortcut!

I ask myself the big question....
is this person my best friend?

PLAY ACTING

I was.... who I was expected to be.
That left me.... behind the curtain,
labeled anonymous.

When I opened the curtain to let me
out.... I found.... that person had
died from a lack of love.

        The New Me?

I'm feeling good. I live, love and I
learned that....

" Play Acting " is not the place to be.

SINGLES

There are many single people in this world, more each day. Some are like fish out of water, trying hard to get with it. Most are apprehensive of getting into the swing of things again. Others appear to be having the time of their life. Probably, they're not. It can be difficult.

It seems like the right person isn't waiting around the corner, but you keep on looking. When you have your courage and your self- esteem back, you may meet someone who recognizes you as one who has made the necessary adjustments. Two fish out of water, do not make a strong pair, two fish that have learned to swim again, do.

So many people are attracted to someone who needs help. They believe that they're going to be the one to "save" them. The idea is to become well first, then go looking for someone who has accomplished the same. That works!

How do you get yourself in shape? It takes determination. You can get counseling, read books on the subject, or join with a group interested in personal wholeness. A recommendation from a reliable source will help you to make your choices on which books or groups. There are also choices in counseling for low income people. The good thing is, there's help for those who want it.

Everyone has a "soap". I've heard an amazing number of stories over the years and each one believes his to be unique. It's usually not. Mine felt unique but it wasn't. It was just another story. Hopefully, you have a good sense of humor; no doubt you'll need it.

We can suffer bodily harm, financial loss, and destruction of our self-esteem, all the rest, and still come through with flying colors.

You have to care enough to put faith in yourself and ask for God's help. When the going gets rough, you'll be fine.

Don't stay home and pout. Go out with a friend and get with it again. My friend Sharon and I go here and there to see what's going on in town. Neither of us drinks, so we have club sodas all evening. Who knows? We enjoy music and that's our entertainment!

Perhaps one of the following stories or mini-essays may strike a chord. I hope one hits you at just the right time. (Timing is everything, you know.) We have to be in an accepting mood, want to do better for ourselves, before we can make it. Everyone makes mistakes. Get over it! Believe that you deserve it, and it will come.

WHAT IS

COURAGE
is what enables me to move forward.

FEAR
is what makes me apprehensive.

HATRED
is what destroys my tranquility.

LOVE
is the healer of all.

THE KEY

A positive attitude is the key to

locking the door

on fears and failures.

TRY SUCCESS

Rather than trying to change

things or other people,

try changing

your own attitude.

There you will find success.

SUGGESTIONS

These are suggestions from me to you in hopes that my well-worn travels on the road to happiness will give you ideas on how to plan your course.

One of my greatest lessons was how to laugh at my own dumb and costly mistakes. I made them "big time" and I'll remember them "big time". That was the whole idea, I'm sure.

Expect surprises. They're built in for your learning process; we all have them. You will find that God too, has a great sense of humor. Funny and strange "coincidences" will happen. But there are no coincidences! Everything happens for a reason. Some day, we may understand. Maybe not! Either way, we can learn how to make our journey an on-going lesson in rediscovering the knowledge with which we were all born. We can learn how to discard the fear of rejection, fear of failure and the fear of not deserving the happiness we hope to find.

    These old wounds need to heal. Let them. We carry them far too long. We can let them go! By dropping these things one- by-one, our travels will be much more pleasant.

SOAPS

Ever think about the soaps in people's lives? We all have them, and try to deal with them the best way we know how. Why do these things happen? Some things can be disastrous, painful and discouraging, Why? Some would say, "Why not?"

So often, we need to correct our faults and willful ways. What I have noticed is, when things repeatedly happen, it's a signal to pay closer attention. If I don't I know that I'll get in trouble again. Repeat lessons work. They get our attention, sooner or later.

My teacher used to ask, "Did you read yesterday's lesson?" We'd all raise our hands and smile. Some of us meant it! It didn't take long for her to sort us out. I was the little tomboy who loved to goof off. I liked to get by with things and never get caught. I always got caught, but I still held on to my habit.

Since then, I've raised four children. That taught me extensive survival tactics that helped when I lost very important people in my life. Plus, I didn't succumb when I also lost all of my material possessions. Isn't it odd, that in the act of losing, I won?

Learning how to pick yourself up and put one foot in front of the other is hard; but it is not impossible. The lessons are difficult. They have to be to get our attention.

There are many ways I've changed my attitude about life, however, not my sense of humor. Humor was an invaluable help. I was able to laugh at my escapades that didn't pan out the way I wanted. I chalked them up to experience and came out the winner. You might question what I won. But, I know all too well what it was: It was me!

All my wars are over. Can you believe it? I do. I've been through the fire and rain. I'm referring now to losing my daughter. A friend clued me in to something important.

She had lived through the same tragedy and realized that now we can live with the knowledge that nothing and no one can ever take us down that far again. Suzie made a special point to call me and share that thought. She's absolutely right.

Add the rest of what happened to me and you have to become convinced. I left without my material possessions and didn't give it a second thought. I said, "I have me." Understand?

Everything gets easy when you get your priorities in order. Someone said that women set limits in their mind and when those limits are exceeded they leave their abusive life. I had two limits and met them head on, all in one night. I feel that whoever said that little gem, knew what they were talking about.

By hard work, over a period of time, I have changed my ways and I'm certain there will be more changes. That's what we're here for, you know. School isn't out until we graduate. And isn't it ironic that graduation day is celebrated by mourning? I picture graduation day as the vacation we all need after struggling with the lessons.

This brings to mind my experience of what is now called, the "near death experience". Believe me, the vacation spot is absolutely beautiful! It's populated with people you used to know. Most everyone.

There's also a Great Welcomer there who was so understanding when I told Him that I couldn't stay because I still had one more son to raise. He understood and said that my friends just wanted to show me around, then I would have to go back. Unbelievable! It was so beautiful. My daughter was there; so lovely and so happy. It did my heart good to nearly die!

The soap goes on, just like the television stories, only we don't have to take it so seriously, and we'd better not. Life can be beautiful. It is, when we get it in our head to write it the way we want it. It *is* our call.

WHO DID IT?

Who did you wrong?

The anger still lives.

Love lost, time too.

How did it feel,
thrown back at you?

Now, you have a constant
companion, whose face
you cannot see.

The present is not the present you
thought it would be.

(Anger is your middle name.)

A controlling force,
strangling your life.

The past is gone.

The present is going.

The future looks dim.

Unmask the villain.

Look in the mirror,
see your reflection.

You betrayed you.

Learn your lesson.

Release the past.

Anger and peace
are not cohabitants!

GROWING PAINS

It's difficult to think of love as being transitory, nevertheless, it has been proven to be so. I loved my childhood; now, it's gone. People and things are here for only an allotted time, but then, so am I.

Getting over the loss of love is called the growing process and never ends. Thank God we can survive the growing pains; never experiencing love would be the worst thing that could happen.

WHO WON?

Divorce can be so disruptive to our state of mind. It controls every facet of our life. Gender has no importance in this matter. It hits male and female alike, without discrimination.

Having mingled with the single set for quite a few years now, I feel like I've heard it all. Everyone has a story. (I call them soaps!) In the beginning, we all feel we shouldn't have to go through this difficult process. And children must not! In the end, we come out with two groups, the winners and the losers. In reality, the winners can be the losers, and the losers can wind up being the winners!

Winning doesn't necessarily connote the person who received the most money or material possessions. Winning describes the person who came out with no bitterness and retained their peace of mind. If this sounds easy, then possibly you've not been in a complicated divorce. Having met men and women who hold the bitterness close to their heart, sometimes forever, I've come to an important conclusion: If, in our mind, we remain to feel threatened, wronged or defeated, then we have lost.

Anger, bitterness, resentment, jealousy, or envy will totally destroy our well being. The irony of it all is...it doesn't effect our ex-wife or husband at all! The sum total is, we're giving away not only the victory and possibly the material possessions----but also our precious peace of mind.

We could gain money and possessions back during our lifetime, but we will never gain back our peace of mind, unless we work on it religiously, starting now.

The road to success on this matter is to love yourself first, then find love for your "opponent". Oh boy, " Easier said than done!" But you can do it and the best way to start is to pray for that person and mean it. We are all trying to find our way through this difficult world. Too many pressures, too much materialism and not enough love in the hearts of fellow men. Compassion for the trials and tribulations of others has gone by the wayside, since we have concentrated on our own egos and desires. It's called "Getting ahead of the game," and it's now the driving force in our society.

Victory in divorce is not about wining things. Victory is about feeling good about yourself and afterwards, letting go of the issues.

Try a new approach to "Getting ahead of the game", by making your game one that's beneficial to you. Love yourself first and regain your peace of mind, then it'll be possible to tolerate the transgressions of others. You'll understand that they also have a lot to learn, <u>in their own time.</u> If you're ready to change your attitude, this may be<u> your time.</u> I sincerely hope so. It's no fun being angry.

YOU MIGHT ASK

Why couldn't we be born with more sense? In fact, there is a theory that we are born with all the basics that we need. Then, somehow, we lose it as we travel down our chosen path. Interesting!

Babies are happy little creatures, yet most are taken care of for their every need by loving parents. Those that aren't so lucky have to make the best of what they have.

Sooner or later, we all find easy ways to get what we want. Then, we have to make choices. Do we want to succumb to greed, lies, cheating or control? I think about the things that were given to me that broke, wore out, disappeared or were stolen. Isn't that strange? The important things I really need do come my way after I'm ready to accept responsibility for them. Then, they last.

I do need friends with a like mind whose values are well placed. They may know exactly where they're going or they may not have a clue. Good people get lost in this material world. We all search. Some know what they're searching for, and some are still questioning. That's okay. It takes time to realize how much love there can be in a lifetime. Or how much help we can be to someone less fortunate.

I want to be as successful as the next person, but it's also important to me to enjoy life. And it's crucial to remain content with my lot. My goal is to be pleased with my life and to show God I do appreciate everything He's given me-------including the problems. They were meant to make me stronger and they did. There were good times, bad times and plenty of opportunities to improve myself. Of course, He knows when to throw in some pretty big perks to keep me in line. He also knows about my willful ways.

What confidence to know we have a Master Teacher who never gives up on his pupil. When there seems to be no easy way out and one comes in the nick of time, out of nowhere----He's there, or when everything looks like it's going down the tubes and it doesn't ----He's there. When you need a laugh and it comes from someone you don't even know or when your hopes are nearly gone and everything turns around in record time---- He's there.

At times, I wonder if He's getting tired of me. I ask for so much. As long as He's willing, I'm game. I'll tell you where he hangs out, if you'd like to know. You can easily find Him. He's with you every minute of the day or night, waiting for you to call Him. Ask and you shall receive.

John   Chapter 16:24

FINDING YOUR BEST FRIEND

The object of your affection should be your best friend. That's not exactly how the old song goes; though it should be your theme song.

Today, too many couples don't take time to find out if they can be best friends. It seems like everyone's in a hurry. Yes, we're all getting older but ye gads Maggie; we're not going to vanish at the stroke of midnight!

Is it desperation, low self-esteem or what? Going to bed with a stranger is done all the time. Sex like that can be compared to exercise, not to caring.

I've not been a prude nor even wise about the subject; however, there comes a time when you have to question yourself on how to best handle this problem. What is the motive? Are we that lonely? Are we that needy? If so, we can get over it. Most of us have been lonely, needy and confused. Let's try to get our mind clear about what it is we want.

After lots of conversations with myself, I know what it is I want. I want to find my best friend. He will care how I feel. He will want me to be sure that there are more than just hormones working, because he too has deep feelings. More than likely, he has also had a few heartaches. Why then, would either of us want to hurt or be hurt again?

Everyone is entitled to a slip up. Still, it's one thing to slip and another to keep on making excuses. Feeling good about our relationship is extremely important. How could we be best friends and not respect one another? Not likely.

Be smart, be above the crowd of aimless wanderers running from one partner to the other. Respect yourself first, then the best will follow. No one can tell someone else how long to wait for the seriousness to start. That has to be between the two people involved. It just might work out better if they at least get to know each other first. Without some time spent together, they're cheating themselves out of the romance.

Competition puts the fear into some and they believe if they don't nail it down now, they'll lose out. Nonsense. Competition will always be there. It's up to us to have confidence in ourselves.

Assuming that everything works out fine, we've made each other happy just being together, sharing thoughts and finding out what we have in common: Things like, what we both want out of this romance. Eventually, we'll also find out how much we mean to each other. These things count.

Good luck in finding your own best

friend. He or she _is_ out there, hoping to find you. And if it's Gods will, you will, because God is the Supreme Best Friend and wants all of us to be happy.

STAGE FRIGHT

Your life is your stage debut.

See that you

write it,

direct it,

and star in it.

Share it with those you love.

EXTRAVAGANZA

About ten years ago, our town had a big celebration featuring many top-notch Country-and-Western groups. Some of my friends said I could go with them and volunteer to help park the vans, buses and cars belonging to the performers. In return, we would get free passes for the performance. That sounded good, so I joined them.

Actually, it was fun parking everyone, waving them on, and telling them where they could or could not park. Control, control! It was great!

About noon, our job was finished and the show was about to start. I grabbed my chair, thermos and purse from the trunk of my car and ran to the stage area. After the ticket taker had my ticket, it was catch -as-catch- can, for a place to sit. I've never seen so many people spread out over so many acres.

After I claimed my spot, I walked around, then stood next to a man who looked overdressed for the occasion. He was in a business suit with shoes that had been polished to a high sheen before he hit the dust of the fairgrounds. In front of us, was a man who wore his Harley ® jacket, jeans, boots and hat. "I wish I could dress like that", the polished man said, as he pointed ahead of us.
"Why can't you", I asked.
"Because I'm an attorney and I have to give a good impression. Anyway, he looks so tough I'd be afraid to talk to him."

After that remark, I left him, to join the "tough guy". We had a long conversation about Harley's ®, his family and his job. He said he no longer rode with the group. I asked him why, and he said that he wanted to live. After he married his wife and had a son, he felt that he should play it a little safer. He no longer drinks or gambles. He seemed to be very content with his decisions. He appeared to be a very happy man, unlike the important lawyer I had just met, who was judging the Harley ® man.

What a scary man, Mr. Attorney!

Never judge a book by it's cover, baby!

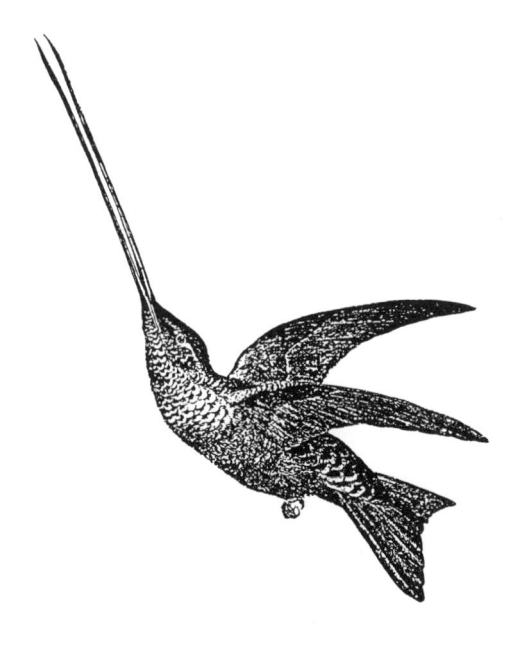

THE TOP 12 LIST

As you can see by now, I've certainly made my mistakes. I've learned to pay attention, simply because---- if I don't---- I'll have to pay for it.

The following is my top 12 list that helps to keep me grounded. Hope you enjoy it. My original copy has a little Gooney bird on it. He has a red and black dunce cap on his head, super large glasses and tissue paper wings! He reminds me of me!

Continued.......

THE TOP 12 LIST

THINGS THAT TAKE FOREVER TO LEARN:

12. HAPPINESS COMES FROM WITHIN.

11. THE ONLY ONE YOU CAN CHANGE IS YOURSELF.

10. IF IT'S WORTHWHILE IT'S PROBABLY NOT EASY.

9. BE GOOD TO YOURSELF AND LOVE IT.

8. KNOWING YOUR SELF-WORTH.

7. WHEN TO START AND WHEN TO QUIT.

6. WORRY IS USELESS.

5. EXCESSES ARE SUBSTITUTES FOR A NEED.

4. MIND YOUR OWN BUSINESS.

3. IF IT'S NOT GOOD, DON'T SAY IT OR DO IT.

2. AVOID MAKING THE SAME MISTAKE TWICE.

1. REMEMBER THE IMPORTANCE OF THESE THINGS.

I'm sure there are more, right? See how many you can do, but not all at one time.

You may have more to add to the list that would better suit your circumstances. Feel free to do so. Personally, that's enough for me.

I've had good luck when I tell people, I never make promises. Then, they know not to expect too much. I never do things for their sake; I do them for me. I get annoyed at myself if I don't succeed. No sense in both of us being upset!

LIFE'S CHOICES

The master stands aside, looks at all things, and realizes his "right choices" were his reward for the knowledge he gained from the past.

His "wrong choices" were merely another chance to learn his lessons.

FRIENDS AND LOVERS

You can be a lover in one evening. Being a tried and true friend takes an investment of time.

Lasting relationships are when you've been through the good and bad times together, and love one another even more. You've accepted your differences, allowed shortcomings, resolved clashing opinions, and still want to be together. I'm not too sure that love doesn't have a middle name: It could be ......Respect.

FIRST THINGS FIRST.

Be kind to yourself,
kinder than you've ever been.

This is the way to start experiencing
the love you're hoping to find.

FINDING A FOCUS

There was a little boy who wanted to explore, question and find the next new adventure. As he grew into a teenager he had the same ambitions. His path was not the ordinary one, but it was by his own design.

Not realizing that his path would be a rocky one, he stuck to his decision and suffered the consequences. As he matured, it became obvious that he had ventured too far in the wrong direction and was lost. He was alone in a crowd of lost wanderers. His desperation became his salvation.

As he traveled on, he found a better path. Better, not because it was less rocky, but because he found friends there in different stages of enlightenment. There were those who were more confused and barely had their eyes open, and there were those who had developed a finer tuning on the importance of one's life choices. He found that he could help those who desperately needed a friend and he met those who could be his helpful friend.

    Wisdom is the product derived from learning and the key to learning is to pay attention. He had found a place to focus on his desire to explore, question, and choose a new adventure. He focused on his life, his choices and his own well being. He became what he had always wanted to be, a lovable human being who had empathy for those who were lost on the path. He earned the respect of others but, more importantly, he respected himself. Finally, his path had become his friend, not his enemy.

OUR CHILDREN

We enjoy our children for their youth and uniqueness. Then, we send them forth into a life of their own choosing, with love and contentment in our hearts.

Their mistakes are their way of learning, as were ours. We must worry not, judge not; each of us falls short of perfection. Our children belong to the world for they are the world's promise of a tomorrow.

MUTUAL

A strange word, mutual. A necessary word when it comes to love relationships. A key word to remember when you're assessing what it is you're calling a caring relationship. How many people are caring? Is it one or two?

Relationships are not easy. They require mutual nurturing. When problems inevitably occur, as they always do, the trick is obvious. You have made the choice. It's no longer just me, it's we. The objective you must always remember is, we will always want what's best for both of us. If that's the shared theme in your relationship ------- you have a treasure.

INDECISION

Indecision is simply stagnation,
the void where nothing can grow.

Fear not, too much gusto
nor modesty.

Instead, fear indecision.
Cowards do not participate in life.

LOVE IS A CHOICE

Love comes and goes
at your direction.

You can ask it to stay,
or make it leave.

You may enjoy it,
 for as long as you choose.

Or....you may fear it,
for as long as you choose.

Or....you may mourn it
for as long as you choose.

It's your choice.

JOHN

John was my childhood sweetheart; we were the best of friends all through school. In my junior year of high school, he went away for the entire summer. He didn't call or write. I thought it was over, and I started dating again. When he returned, he found that I was no longer available. I was dating someone else.

I really don't believe in mistakes, however, it's difficult to see why we couldn't have spent our lifetime together. We certainly were compatible and had so much fun together. Eventually, we both faced some pretty hard lessons. Separately, we built our lives, which ended in divorces.

After I had filed for my divorce, I called him and we got together. What a shock it was to both of us, after not seeing each other for more than 30 years. We were no longer the carefree teens who couldn't wait to be together. Still, we were the same two people, feeling the same way about each other.

We moved into his mobile home. After a year, we built our own new home. Life for both of us was never so good. It lasted over three years. Then, he began to have strokes, one after the other. Later, his relatives said, they knew he had suffered a personality change. I didn't know what was wrong. I knew things were not the same.

One morning he looked at me so sadly. He said he thought we should break up. My divorce was still not completed, we were never married. I left the next morning and returned to my hometown.

After a few weeks, he said he had made a terrible mistake. I refused to go back. I was so hurt. Two years later, his condition had gradually become worse and he had to have people in to care for him. By then, I was engaged to a very good man. We met at a dance and got along very well together. Every so often, Dick didn't mind if I went to see

Every so often, Dick didn't mind if I went to see John; he knew it made him happy to see me.

The last time I talked to John he was being driven home from Florida. The woman who took care of him had called and asked if I'd like to talk to him. She didn't think he would make it home.

Because of the strokes, John had not been able to speak more than three or four words for several years. I led the conversation, knowing that his reply could only be yes or no. My last words to him were, that I had always loved him and always would. He said his simple yes. He died before he got back home.

John was also a victim of the divorce courts and had vowed not to marry again. Me too. I was still afraid. We made a good pair.

I didn't go through with my marriage plans and ended the long engagement. It was then that I realized, I needed to get straightened out in my head. My fears had prevented me from ever finding the happiness I wanted.

It's been a long haul, but progress has been made. I feel in control of my life and can now plan my future. I don't have those gloomy black clouds hanging over me anymore. I realize that there will be ups and downs; now I'm equipped to handle them.

John always wanted me to write about our love story. It was a sweet, funny, exciting and loving time. It was all that one could ask for. Someday, I may put it all down on paper. For now, I can only say he was the best friend I've ever had.

When we were 12 years old, the teacher came into the room with him and introduced him to the class. I looked up from my book and saw a blonde, good looking boy wearing blue jeans. I made up my mind right then to get to know him. I wasted no time because I really liked what I saw. He was for me and I knew it.

After that day, we were friends. He would come to my house and I'd spend a lot of time at his house, talking to him and his mother.

Four years later, we had the green light from my parents, to start dating. There were some romantic times and some adventurous times. He had a motor scooter and we'd be on it every chance we got.

I remember the day he told me he was going to Texas for the summer. I was so sad. Little did I know, that was the beginning of the end. It would be more than 30 years until we got back together.

We had three and a half wonderful years. I have regrets that my pride kept us apart near the end. But it was meant to be, another big lesson.

SO MUCH MORE TO SAY

I wanted to tell him how much he meant to me, but I didn't. I thought he would know.

We talked about everything but not about that. Time slipped by.

I didn't realize he had the same fears. Now he's gone, forever.

I'm no longer afraid of rejection. I'm afraid I'll never get a second chance.

Now, I wouldn't wait to express my feelings.

There was so much more to say.

MOTHER AND DAD

What a stormy life my mother and dad had. Then one day, after my wedding, they ended their marriage. That was the start of new beginnings for them.

Dad remarried first, then Mother found her man. It worked out very well for all of them. Many years went by with lots of happiness. Years later, Mother was left a widow and found a way to go on. She kept busy running her antique shop and playing bingo on the side.

We spent quite a bit of time together, over the years. She moved a lot and after one of those moves she became ill with what her doctor said was bronchitis. He was wrong. Mother called me early on a Sunday morning and said she had a difficult time trying to sleep with her terrible cough. It had been going on too long. I took her to the emergency room where they x-rayed her immediately.

The next morning she told me she had been diagnosed with lung cancer. That night, I prayed that the doctors were wrong. They were not. When I had to accept the facts, I prayed she would not suffer. The cancer had spread and attached to the bones. The doctors told me it would be very painful. Mother had no pain. She didn't need any pain medicine or shots for the duration of her illness. The doctors and nurses found it hard to believe; I found it to be my miracle. The outcome was not what I'd asked for the first time, however, it was God's will not mine, and it was the help that was needed.

I thank God for His mercy on my mother who never doubted that He would help her. Amazing.

That was in 1984. Now Dad has also been alone for the past four years. He's no longer able to walk without help. He's in Florida with my younger half-brother and his family. Dad's losing his will to stay in this, his empty world. Work was everything to him and he was good at it. I hope and pray to God my Dad doesn't suffer on this, the last leg of his journey.

My parents were good to me even though, when together, they had major problems. They did the best that they knew how, at that time. Later in life, they tried to make up for the stormy times we had. And they did. They showed me that they loved me. It wasn't too late.

JUDGMENTS

Did you ever stop to think what this world would be like if people didn't make judgments on each other? Nice!

When you decide that someone is not doing right, instead of criticizing, realize you are not his or her judge. Your opinion is just that: Your opinion. It's not necessarily correct and probably not wanted.

Proof is usually elusive when we make judgments on others. We assume. We assume we know what the situation is, when we don't. We assume we are right, when we don't know all the facts. We assume we know outcomes. We don't. How did we get so much smarter than everyone else?

We didn't........ let's do our own homework!

PRIORITY LIST

First, review your priority list. Change it, until it looks right for you.
Have everything just so.

Now........... you know!

OUTCOMES

How easy and unreliable it is to depend upon outcomes.

An outcome is not determined by what you wish it to be.

An outcome is the result of what is.

Depend upon your own direction. You'll be more in charge.

JOHN 13-34

LOVE ONE ANOTHER.

HOW SIMPLE.

HOW CHALLENGING.

HOW EASY TO FORGET.

THE KEYS

They say the key to happiness and success is....

"One Day At A Time."

Isn't it worth a try when our pockets are filled with keys that just won't fit?

EVERYONE SHOULD HAVE A BIRDSHIRT

What would a birdshirt be? It might be a shirt you could put on when you'd like to be someplace else. Wouldn't it be a nice thing to have after you've said the wrong thing to the wrong person?

Wouldn't it be fun to fly, just like in your best dreams? But before you know it, some smart guy would think of a way to market them! They'd be everywhere. Can you imagine how crowded the airways would be? And how confused the birds would feel?

Let's stick it out without the shirt, if not for the sake of the birds, for the sake of you and I, in learning how to cope.

OUR FREE CHOICE

God gave us the freedom to choose our own path and the right to pursue it to the best of our ability.

We make our choices based on what we think we can do.

Each day, we can review our choices.

Each day, we may choose again.

Isn't that generous?

OUR RIGHTS

God gave us the right to choose

for ourselves.......

not for others.

DISAPPOINTED

Dreams shattered, fallen to the ground.

It's okay to cry out loud.

Sorrow must be felt and known.

Dream again....soon.

SPRING'S LESSON

Spring is here once again. The birds are chirping, loving, and building their nests. Wonder how long the lease is? She's in for a long stay. He's getting ready for the food search. Their lives go the way they always knew it would.

We have choices. We are liable to make errors. Sometimes, we want too much out of life and when expectations aren't met....it's not good.

Acceptance is needed if you want to stay content with your progress. Always wanting, sometimes achieving ------- may prove to be upsetting. Live within your comfort zone; then, you can enjoy life just as the little birds do.

LIFE'S SONG

The music of life hits high notes
and low notes. It was never
 intended to be monotonous.

The song goes on, never ending
........taking with it, only those
 who appreciate it's unique melody.

MEMORIES

Memories are like yesterday's newspaper.

It was interesting; it had good news and bad.

Review your good memories for pleasure.

Review your bad ones, only for learning.

MOTHER

Mother was a beautiful woman who never looked or acted her age. After she had passed away, everyone said, "What a lovely lady."
She had married Dad when she was 21 and couldn't know it wouldn't last. There were many hard times with that marriage, too many for it to survive. I likened their marriage to oil and water. They just don't mix. When divorce was offered as a solution to their problems, I was in total agreement.

As fate would have it, Mother was happy with her life when she became ill. We had gotten very close to each other. She had her business, friends, relatives, and me to keep her busy.

No one, including me, gave Mother enough credit for having her act together. She was a very smart, caring lady who loved her family. I apologize for not seeing that, until it was almost too late. Love you.

WHAT'S WRONG?

Everything needs attention in order to grow. Love isn't exempt. Can you be so certain that your relationship is not in need of a little confirmation? Are you feeling and looking the best way possible? Or, are you too busy like the ants in my story? Think about it.

Learn how to work through your problems by not over- reacting. Jumping to conclusions has been my downfall. I always think I know what's going to happen next. I don't. Now that I've put it into God's hands it works much better.(Unless I have a relapse and take it back.) It happens!

This method works for all situations. Love, business, rearing children, making money, and most anything. Why? Because God doesn't make mistakes-------we do.

DIRECTION

Life has been interesting to say the least. I don't know where it's going next or how it will work out. If it were up to me to direct it, I would be worried. I'm learning to take things as they come, not make assumptions and try not to control the people involved. It's been a long lesson. In the past, I've been the director, star, writer and editor. Needless to say, it was not good.

I study, weigh and evaluate all things now. As some would say, "Chew on it for awhile." Jumping to action is not good. It has caused me a great deal of pain.

Possibly, you will be a quick study, I wasn't. My parents used to say I was a stubborn little girl. I was. But life has a way of cutting you down to size. Arrogance is not attractive. Wilfulness is not either. I think I was guilty. Or maybe I was putting on my armor so I couldn't be hurt.

We try to avoid being hurt. We are not always successful in our efforts. I've made some small and large errors in judgment, and also had to pay for them. Not by sitting in my room, as when I was a child, but by feeling guilt-ridden with my conscience hurting.

As an adult there is no parent to apologize to or tell that I'm going to do better. There are no deals to be made. There's just a promise to myself that I'll try harder next time.

Are we infallible? God knows we're not.

Life is hard. Life can change and does quite often. The changes are for the better when you're serious about knuckling down and getting to work on your issues.

Sometimes, I'm tired. I'm tired of trying so hard to absorb lessons. I ask God to make it clear what He wants me to do. I don't actually hear His answer, however, there are times when I know exactly what He wants me to do. It's like a knowing, not spoken words, just thoughts transmitted. Strange. And always correct. When things pile up, I sometimes ask Him if I could go on a vacation. Just a little time off. Most always, it's okay. Then I'm refreshed and life is beautiful again.

We have our life, our children, our friends and those who travel the course. We are all on the path going as fast as we can. Some have gotten careless and are going in the wrong direction, not that they have to stay there. God willing, we will all find the way.

TEDDY

Three year old Teddy lives on a dead end street with a circle at the end. This spring day he was riding his red tricycle. He was moving pretty well, legs going faster and faster. As he looked up, he saw his friend Billy up in the tree in the center of the circle. Billy is ten and adventurous.

A look of wonderment came over Teddy's face and he yelled, "Billy, Billy, how did you get up there? Did you ----Fly?"

....

No, we can't fly. Just a little hard work gets us where we want to go.

GET IT OUT

"When there's something bothering you, get it out." That's the advice I got from my stepmother Ethel, quite some time ago. She said she never held back and confronted whoever said or did the irritating thing. She didn't waste any time letting it fester. She was right.

Anytime you can talk things out, you're way ahead of the game. Talking is important in all kinds of relationships. If you can't discuss, you can't resolve. Everything is at a dead end when there's no communication. Then, frustration sets in. Following that, resentment. It grows into a monumental thing.

You may be the talker or you may be the quiet one. It matters not which you are, the fact remains that you're in a bind. These things can be worked out with adults. The problem arises when one party can not be an adult. It's best to grow up!

CUTTING SLACK

Do you remember the saying, "Cutting him some slack"? It means to give someone a little room to move in, or to make allowance for errors. I would hope my family and friends cut me some slack. At times, I need it. I do it for them, no matter if they realize it or not.

I've made judgments on people and ruined our relationships. Paying for that error was very hard. Did I learn the first time? You guessed it....no. Recently, I started to do it again. Fortunately, I corrected my impulsive behavior and didn't act in haste. You can see I've always had a lot to work on.

Wonder how I got so off track? Most ot the time, I believe I acted out of self-protection. The fear of being slighted, tricked or controlled urged me on. I forgot. Now, it's a friendlier world I've made for myself.

ATTENTION

Everything needs attention in order to grow. Love isn't exempt. This holds true for any relationship. Tend to yourself first, so you can give freely to those you love.

There seems to be more interest now in telling someone you love them. There was a time when people didn't. It seemed too hard to get it out. Emotions were not a big topic of conversation. Today, they are. And that's helped to save many a relationship.

All of us need attention from each other. Studies show if babies are held and loved, they can grow into loving people. Neglected babies do not fare well. We are not unlike babies. We are bigger, sometimes we're smarter, sometimes not! So, put more love into your life....it's wonderful! You'll find out for yourself.

TOMORROW

"Tomorrow is promised to no one."

A friend quoted that to me long ago. I don't know who said it, but he was unquestionably correct. Time does have a habit of flying by. One day you're young, then you're not!

When you're young, this quote would have little effect on you, since time is not flying. I used to smile, listen, then go on my merry way. Now, it's a different story.

We can't roll back the clock.
We can make certain we treasure each day.
We can work on making the right choices for ourselves from now on.
We can get rid of negative thinking habits like:
"EASIER SAID THAN DONE."
Can't we?

TRAGEDIES

These last pages are dedicated to parents who have lost a child. Others may want to read it also. As with all of the previous subjects, I have lived through this one too. This, without question, is the most difficult lesson in the book of life.

I first wrote about this in 1985 and it tore me apart. Eight years had passed and it seemed like yesterday. Now, thirteen years have gone by and, in some ways, it still seems like yesterday. I miss her so much. We didn't have the time together I planned on. We were going to be shopping buddies; lunch on the patio, movies together and I would be her confidant for relating her dating stories.

Eventually, there would have been the most beautiful grandchildren; she was a beauty. It didn't happen. All of my hopes, plans and dreams for her were gone.

I can write about this now, only because I know there's more to this life than we know or can prove. Could it ever be proved?

I'm certain in my own mind; there is a life after death. My daughter is around me quite often, even though I can't see her or talk to her. Many times, I feel her presence. She's looking out for me, and knows that I love to be looked after by her. She also knows that I'm not as quick to jump in the wrong direction as I once did, which helps to make her job a little easier.

We will see our children again.
God knows that we will.
He is the Perfect God who loves us.

LEFT BEHIND

My daughter Margie was killed at the age of twenty-two by a drunk driver. It would not have made any difference had she been two or fifty-two; I would still miss her. Had she been ill, lingering on, or as she went, in one split second, there would have been no more or less pain for my family and me.

Children should not leave before their parents; sometimes they do. If your child has left you behind, I'm sorry that you have to have this pain in your heart. There is no quick fix. There is no complete fix, period. There is relief after some time. And everyone has his own time schedule.

After the news came that she had been killed, all I did was walk around and around in the house, throwing my arms up into the air and letting them drop as if in helpless despair. That's exactly what it was.

I wish I had words that would help you, I don't. The only thing I can offer is what was told to me by my youngest child at the time.

Jim was ten years old and trying, like me, to cope. Neither of us was succeeding. However, he had the presence of mind to tell me something that brought me back to reality.

He was sitting at our kitchen table sobbing as he watched me walking and crying. I had been doing this for two or maybe three weeks, and doing nothing else. Hoping to get through to me, he said, " Mother, Margie wouldn't want you to be this unhappy, please stop crying." That did it. It registered and I knew he had spoken the truth. She would not have wanted to see this happen to us. Never in a million years, would she have condoned this misery that we were going through.

Nothing that anyone else said during that whole time made sense to me, except that. The truth came from my child who was feeling his own pain, as he tried to help.

Time does heal and time teaches you how to go on, when you're left behind. I borrow this wisdom from Jim whenever I meet someone who's in the throes of one of the worst times in their life. I have nothing else to give that could possibly make more sense.

Only when I meet someone who has been through this, do I believe they truly understand. Your imagination will not take you to such a hell as what you go through when this happens.

Your whole world crashes before your eyes. It seems that there's nothing left. Nothing matters. The next morning, when you open your eyes and you remember, you go through it again. I wondered if it would never end. I spent most of each day thinking about the tragic ending of a beautiful, young girl. She had just graduated from college and found a job. Things were going well for her.

Now it was all over. Everything was over. I couldn't bear it. Why couldn't it have been me? I wouldn't have minded at all, to go on to a more peaceful place. I had lived for quite awhile, and she was just starting out. It wasn't right.

    Wishing doesn't make it so. Nothing was going to change. I went through each day barely knowing what I was doing. I don't remember most of those first few weeks. Numb is good. Numb doesn't hurt. You just walk and talk and do the best you can.

    Margie and I were never going to be together again. She would never be the bride or mother. I would never see her children. This couldn't be the end. I couldn't stop thinking.

    This went on for quite some time, then one day I put on a pair of slacks and they fell off, dropping to the floor. I hadn't been eating, sleeping or taking care of myself. My doctor told me I was dying. He said he should put me in the hospital, though, he thought it would only make matters worse by being away from my family.

After that, I tried to eat and take better care of myself. Jimmy, my youngest son was depending on me. He needed me to be there for him and I tried.

Gradually, I got with it again; however, each night when I tried to get to sleep, the same scenario would play in my head. The telephone would ring, I'd answer it, and the officer would tell me about the accident, then he would say, "She's dead."
Each night the same thing happened. The telephone call, my answering it, his voice; on it went. This happened for almost a year.

I knew I couldn't stand this much longer, something had to be done. I had an idea. I didn't know if it would work, but I had to try. That night, the phone call came and I refused to answer it. I had to do this less than a week; it has never played out again. Finally, I wore myself out!

Life has gone on for all of us; my three boys are finding their way on their chosen paths. There are three grandchildren now, and who knows how many more there will be? Good kids, smart and all talented in their individual ways.

We talk about Margie and how independent she was, determined not to take anything from anyone. Her short life had more meaning to more people than we ever knew. If ever there was something that's easier said than done, this is it. Nevertheless, I know that you will find peace, once again. You will find your way to resuming your everyday life. You will laugh again. You will cry again. You will love again.

God knows no favorites---- He gives to all, because we are all deserving of His peace.

TO BEREAVED PARENTS

By now, you know you have had the hardest lesson in life, and you must go on. I was not a very religious person before Margie died. I am now, in a different way. I have had my vision opened by supernatural events. I didn't ask for them, they came to me totally unexpected. These things were brought to me by God for the sole purpose of giving me the gift of knowing there's more here than we see. More than likely, it had to be that dramatic for me to pay attention.

There was a period of time when the "Angel" came to me and told me many things. I use the word angel because people understand angels. Actually, he was not an angel. As I understand it, angels have never lived here on earth. They may visit, but they were not born here. This person was born here 100 years ago, and he is what is now called a guide. I am not a psychic; I did not see him. I did "listen" to him. There was not a voice; there was a knowing. He said he was sent by God to help me. God knows I needed help.

I do believe his coming brought me out of my utter despair. The guide said that Margie also had something to do with the visit. It must have disturbed her immensely to see me like that. When Jim told me she wouldn't want me to be so unhappy, that had to be her wish.

If you will keep your loved one's wishes in mind, you will go on with your life. We can never forget their leaving, although we can learn to accept it for what it was. It was time for that person to go to a better place. Their job was done; they accomplished what they came to do.

A child is born into this world for a reason. If he only stays for less than a second, his presence here is never forgotten. It's beyond us to try to understand these things. God knows the answers, and someday we may too.

I believe the "Angel". See if you could reason it out in your mind that your child would feel badly about making you so sad. I think it's absolutely correct. Even if you didn't have the best relationship with your child, it stands to reason, your child understands more now. And we will too, when we get to where we're going.

After the visit from my guide, I felt greatly relieved to know that Margie still lives. I can't see her or go there, but someday I will. Eternity is a long time; our time here is short.

We must go on. God wants to help us go on and be content. Life <u>will</u> return to a happier state, as soon as you permit it. Mourning is needed by all that are left behind. Do it. Then live your life---- knowing---- there really is no end. We are all here for an allotted time, for a specific purpose. When we leave, we will see our children again. Ask God for a peaceful mind to carry you through.

His promise: "Ask and you shall receive."